Copyright Page

Table of Contents

Foreword

Introduction: The Poison We Choose

Foreword

Some books entertain you. Others inform you. But occasionally, a book arrests your soul, confronts your truths, and invites you to break free from the very thing that's been holding you hostage, and it is often without you even knowing it. *Unforgiveness: A to Z* is one of those rare books.

This is not a light read. This is not a casual devotional. This is spiritual surgery. It peels back the layers of hidden pain, suppressed emotion, and silent suffering caused by one of the most toxic forces in the human experience: unforgiveness. With raw honesty, spiritual depth, and compassionate precision, this work explores how unforgiveness weaves itself into our emotions, our minds, our bodies, our relationships and even our faith.

From **Anger** to **Zero Peace**, every chapter in this book serves as both a mirror and a map. A mirror, to show us where unforgiveness may be lurking beneath the surface of our lives. A map, to guide us out of the fog and into the freedom that only forgiveness can bring.

But make no mistake about it, this is a war for your soul. It is easier to stay angry. It is safer to stay guarded. It is more convenient to pretend the past didn't shape the present. But you will never become all God has called you to be while shackled to what someone else did to you.

This book is not about excusing evil or pretending pain didn't happen. It's about reclaiming your peace, your power, and your purpose. It's about learning how to let go and not so that they can go free, but so that *you* can.

If you're ready to walk into emotional, spiritual, and relational wholeness...then turn the page.

Introduction: The Poison We Choose

Imagine drinking poison every single day and expecting the other person to die. Sounds foolish, right? Yet, this is exactly what unforgiveness does, it slowly kills us from the inside out while the person who hurt us often moves on, unaware or unaffected.

Unforgiveness is a silent thief. It robs us of joy, steals our peace, and chains us to a past we can't change. It disguises itself as protection, whispering, "If you let go, they win." But in reality, the only person losing is you.

Most of us have been hurt. Some wounds are fresh; others are decades old. Maybe it was betrayal, rejection, abuse, or abandonment. Maybe the person who hurt you never apologized, or worse, they functioned as if nothing happened. The pain is real. The anger is real. But here's the hard truth: holding on to it won't change what happened, it will only change you, and not for the better.

Unforgiveness breeds bitterness, anger, resentment, and even physical sickness. It hardens our hearts and distorts our view of life. And yet, we cling to it, believing that if we let go, we are excusing the wrongdoing. But forgiveness isn't about excusing the offense; it's about freeing yourself from its grip.

This book is about exposing unforgiveness for the deadly force it is. Each chapter will reveal a different consequence of holding on - A for Anger, B for Bitterness, C for Contempt...all the way to Z. By the end, my prayer is that you will not only see the damage unforgiveness causes but also find the strength to release it. Because the truth is, holding on hurts more than letting go.

Are you ready to break free?

A – Anger: The Fire That Burns Within

Scripture to Reflect On: Ephesians 4:26–27, James 1:19–20

Anger is one of the first emotions we experience when we've been wronged. It's natural, it's powerful, and when left unchecked, it's destructive. Unforgiveness fuels anger, turning it into a fire that consumes our thoughts, emotions, and relationships.

1. Anger is not the problem. It's what you ***do*** with it.

> *"Be angry, and sin not..." (Eph. 4:26)*

Anger is not a sin; it's a signal. The problem is not the emotion, it's the execution.

God gave you the capacity to feel anger, but not the *permission* to live in it. What was meant to warn you has now become what's *warring* against you!

You're not wicked because you feel anger. But you are in danger if you let it linger.

2. Unforgiveness is the gasoline. Anger is just the match.

Unforgiveness doesn't just *feed* anger—it **fuels** it. That fire in your chest? That restlessness in your sleep? That inability to love deeply or trust freely? That's not just stress—it's *spiritual smoke* from a fire you haven't put out.

You're not burning bridges, you're burning **yourself**. The bridge to your peace. The bridge to your next blessing. All up in flames because you keep hugging your hatred.

3. The **Weight** of Carrying Anger: You're Strong, But You're Tired

- **Broken relationships**: You're isolating people who didn't even hurt you because you're still mad at the one who did.

- **Poor health**: Your blood pressure isn't high because of salt, it's high because of *bitterness*!

- **Emotional exhaustion**: You're not only tired, you're *tormented*.

- **A hardened heart**: You can't even cry anymore. That's not strength. That's *scar tissue*.

You're not "guarding your heart"—you're burying it. And calling it wisdom."

4. Breaking Free: Four Steps to Fireproof Your Spirit

Acknowledge the hurt

Stop faking spiritual strength. *Faith doesn't deny pain, it confronts it.*

God can't heal what you won't *reveal*. You're bleeding internally but still smiling externally. That's not deliverance, that's denial!

Identify the root

Surface anger is deceptive. Is it really *them*? Or are they just the latest trigger to your unresolved trauma?

If you trace the flame, you'll find the wick. Was it your father's absence? Your ex's betrayal? The friend who lied? The church that mishandled you? Stop lighting candles for people who left you in the dark!

Choose release over revenge

> "Vengeance feels like power—until it poisons your purpose."

You're not weak for walking away. You're wise. Holding onto anger doesn't make you powerful, it makes you *predictable*. And the enemy will keep playing you like a piano because he knows which key triggers your fire.

> "Forgiveness isn't letting them off the hook— it's about getting your spirit *off the leash*."

Seek healing through forgiveness

Please hear me when I say,

> "They may never say sorry. They may never admit what they did. But hear me, you don't need their apology to get your peace. You need *your permission*."

Healing is your job, not theirs. You keep waiting on closure, but God is waiting on choice. You must choose to be healed!

Final Charge: Will You Keep Feeding the Fire?

Anger doesn't stay where you left it—it grows. It leaks into your parenting. It infects your worship. It contaminates your calling.

You can't be *anointed and angry, saved, and stuck, gifted and grudging* and think you're going to walk in freedom.

Let it go! Not because they deserve it. But because *you do*.

Reflect, Release & Realign

What did this chapter reveal about your own heart?

Have you experienced this behavior or emotion in your own life? How has it affected you or others?

Who or what do you need to forgive—past or present—to break free from this?

What truth from God's Word stood out most in this chapter? How can you apply it?

What steps can you take this week to walk in forgiveness and healing?

B – Bitterness: The Root That Corrupts

Scripture To Reflect On: Hebrews 12:15, Ephesians 4:31

Bitterness is what happens when anger is left unchecked. It doesn't just stay in one area of your life...it spreads, poisoning everything in its path. A bitter heart turns love into resentment, joy into cynicism, and trust into suspicion.

1. Bitterness is not just a feeling, it's a fungus.

> *"See to it that no bitter root grows up to cause trouble and defile many..." (Heb. 12:15)*

Bitterness doesn't just live in your heart—it *grows* there. And like mold behind the walls, it may be invisible at first, but it's contaminating the whole house.

You can't speak in tongues in church and speak in spite at home and call it *growth*! Bitterness doesn't just block blessings—it *breeds* toxicity.

2. You thought time would heal it—but time just buried it deeper.

Bitterness is what happens when *time* passes but *truth* never confronts. You didn't forgive, you *forgot*. And now you've got resentment sitting in your spirit with its feet kicked up like it pays rent.

You didn't get over it, you just stopped talking about it. But bitterness doesn't die in silence. It festers.

3. Bitterness: The Silent Killer of the Soul

Here's how you know bitterness is rotting your spiritual roots:

- **Constant negativity**: Every joy is filtered through pain. You can't even enjoy a win—you expect it to turn into a loss.
- **Lack of joy**: You smile out of manners, not out of meaning.
- **Distrust of others**: Everybody feels like a threat when you're still bleeding from betrayal.
- **Emotional numbness**: You're not at peace, you're paralyzed.

"Bitterness don't make you wise—it just makes you *weary*. And now you're suspicious of blessings and allergic to joy."

How to Uproot Bitterness

1. Recognize the damage

You've been blaming them, but bitterness is breaking *you*. Your body is sick. Your spirit is heavy. Your joy is gone. Your relationships are shallow. That's not life, it's slow spiritual suicide.

> "You're not bitter because you're broken— you're bitter because you never healed. And now, everything good must climb over a fence of pain just to reach you."

Ask:

- What have I lost by being bitter?
- What have I missed while I was too busy sulking?

2. Stop rehearsing the pain

You're not reflecting—you're *reliving*. And every time you replay the offense, bitterness gets another breath of life.

> "Some of y'all aren't hurt, you're *hostage*.
> You feed your pain like a pet, then wonder
> why it follows you everywhere."

Start starving the narrative. When it rises up, *shut it down*—with truth, with Scripture, with worship.

3. Make a conscious decision to forgive

Not a feeling. A *decision*. And you might have to make it *every day* until your feelings line up with your faith.

Write the letter. Burn it. Speak the forgiveness. Cry if you must—but *let it go*. Because if you don't, it'll keep growing roots until you can't tell the difference between your trauma and your personality.

Forgiveness is freedom. It's a jailbreak from a prison you've been guarding with pride.

4. Replace bitterness with gratitude

You can't be bitter and grateful at the same time. One displaces the other. Gratitude is not fluff—it's *warfare*. It realigns your soul with heaven.

Thank God until your attitude shifts. Thank Him until your tongue changes. Gratitude is how you *drown the root* before it devours your garden.

Final Charge: Bitterness is a *Trap*, Not a Tool

It makes you feel like you're in control, but in reality—

it's controlling *you*. You think you're guarding your heart, but really, you're *building a prison*.

You're not protecting yourself—you're punishing yourself. You're drinking the poison and waiting on them to die.

It's time. Uproot it. Cut it out at the root. Cry if you must. Scream if you need to. But don't stay in that dark place another day.

> **Healing isn't easy—but neither is being bitter. So which pain are you going to choose?**

Reflect, Release & Realign

What did this chapter reveal about your own heart?

Have you experienced this behavior or emotion in your own life? How has it affected you or others?

Who or what do you need to forgive—past or present—to break free from this?

What truth from God's Word stood out most in this chapter? How can you apply it?

What steps can you take this week to walk in forgiveness and healing?

C – Contempt: The Silent Assassin of Compassion

Scripture to Reflect On: Luke 18:9, Romans 12:3

Contempt is what happens when bitterness ferments. It's not just anger anymore. It's disgust. It's the belief that the one who hurt you is beneath you, unworthy of grace, love, or redemption. Contempt doesn't just change how you see the offender; it changes how you see the world and yourself.

1. Contempt isn't just how you see *them*—it's proof you've lost sight of *Him*.

> *"To some who were confident of their own righteousness and looked down on everyone else, Jesus told this parable..."* (Luke 18:9)

Contempt is not just bitterness evolved—it's bitterness *with a crown on its head*. It's the judgment seat you sat on without the qualifications.

You may not cuss them out...but if you *roll your eyes*, if you *cut them off*, if you *smirk at their downfall*—you're not healed. You're *haughty*.

This is not holiness, it's hidden hostility. And hidden sin is still *sin*.

2. Bitterness builds walls. Contempt builds thrones.

Bitterness hurts. Contempt *hardens*. When you move from *what they did to you*...to *who you believe they are*...you've crossed into contempt.

> "You're not angry anymore—you're acting like judge, jury, and executioner. But don't

forget—you were once on trial too. And God *pardoned* you."

3. The Danger of a Hardened Heart

Let's get real. Contempt is a slow rot. It doesn't always shout, it *smirks*. It doesn't always curse, it *cuts*. You may not throw punches, but you throw shade with surgical precision.

Signs:

- **Dismissive of pain**: "They're just playing victim."

- **Sarcastic mocking**: "Oh, *poor them...* must be hard living with a conscience."

- **Resentment cloaked in righteousness**: "I'm just standing on truth!" (No, you're standing on *ego*.)

- **Wishing failure**: Secretly hoping they suffer? That's not spiritual maturity, that's spiritual rot.

  "You used to cry for souls. Now you celebrate when people fall. That is not God—it's *ego in a robe.*"

Overcoming Contempt Before It Overcomes You

1. Acknowledge your pride

Contempt thrives in comparison. It says, "*I'd never do what they did.*" But Romans 12:3 says *don't think more highly of yourself than you ought.*

  "Some of y'all forgot you were on God's most-wanted list. And now you think you're His personal assistant."

Repentance isn't just for the fallen—it's for the *forgetful.*

2. Humanize the offender

You don't have to excuse the offense to *remember their humanity.* They're broken, just like you.

> "They may have stabbed you with a knife. But ask God, 'What *cut* them first?'"

Seeing people through the lens of compassion doesn't weaken your boundaries, it *strengthens your soul.*

3. Ask God to restore your empathy

> "You can't call yourself 'saved' and be numb to suffering."

Compassion doesn't mean co-signing sin. It means remembering that *mercy* came looking for *you,* even when you were the villain in someone else's story.

> "If your salvation made you mean, bitter, or judgmental—you didn't meet Jesus. You met religion."

4. Practice humility in thought and speech

What you say when they're not in the room reveals your true healing level. Check your tone. Check your heart.

> "It's not about talking nice—it's about *thinking holy.* Sometimes the nastiest words never leave your mouth, but they still rot your soul."

Catch yourself. Shut your mouth if your heart isn't right. Speak life even when you want to spit venom.

That's not fake—that's *formation*.

Final Charge: Contempt is emotional arrogance wrapped in religious justification

You don't need to win. You need to *release*. Because the longer you live with contempt, the more you become the very thing you once hated.

> "You think contempt makes you powerful—but it makes you *pitiful*. You're playing God, and the real God is watching."

Let God *humble* you before He has to *expose* you. And let compassion re-enter your heart—not because they deserve it, but because you refuse to be ruled by hate dressed up as holiness.

Reflect, Release & Realign

What did this chapter reveal about your own heart?

Have you experienced this behavior or emotion in your own life? How has it affected you or others?

Who or what do you need to forgive—past or present—to break free from this?

What truth from God's Word stood out most in this chapter? How can you apply it?

What steps can you take this week to walk in forgiveness and healing?

D – Depression: The Weight That Won't Lift

Scripture to Reflect On: Psalm 34:18, Isaiah 61:3

Unforgiveness is a heavy burden—and when carried long enough, it often turns into depression. The lingering sadness, the emotional numbness, the quiet hopelessness that follows you everywhere is often rooted in unresolved pain. We must learn that depression doesn't always scream; sometimes, it whispers, "Nothing will ever change."

1. Unforgiveness doesn't just break your heart, it breaks your **hope**.

> *"The Lord is close to the brokenhearted and saves those who are crushed in spirit."*
> *(Psalm 34:18)*

Listen, I will say this:

"Some of you are not just sad—you're *spiritually suffocating*. And it isn't just chemical—it's *cumulative*. You deal with years of swallowed pain, rehearsed wounds, and emotional lockdown. And now, you're wearing a smile but living in a fog."

2. Depression isn't always loud, it's the silent funeral for joy.

> "You didn't just lose motivation—you buried it. You didn't just lose interest—you *grieved it to death*."

Unforgiveness is not passive, it's *poisonous*. You've been carrying pain for so long that sadness feels normal. You're not lazy—you're *leaking*. Leaking from a wound you refused to treat.

You're not tired of life. You're tired of *fighting pain alone.*

3. The Emotional Toll of Holding On

Let's be honest:

- **Persistent sadness**: That cloud isn't from the weather—it's from *what you've been carrying.*
- **Withdrawal**: You're not introverted—you're *injured*. And isolation feels safer than rejection.
- **Sleep disruption**: Your mind won't shut up because your soul won't shut down.
- **Loss of purpose**: You didn't stop dreaming. You just stopped *believing you deserved it.*

"When you hold on to what broke you, you build a house with no windows. No light. No air. No joy."

Steps Toward Emotional Healing

1. Name what hurts

Depression is vague on the surface but *surgical underneath*. It's not always "I'm sad"—it's:

- "I never heard 'I'm sorry.'"
- "I didn't get closure."
- "They moved on like nothing happened."

You can't heal what you won't *name*. Stop saying, 'I'm fine.' Say, 'I'm *fractured.*

That name—the one that still makes your stomach turn—is the place your healing begins.

2. Stop carrying the blame

You think it was your fault. You tell yourself:

- "I should've known better."
- "I should've stopped it."
- "Maybe I deserved it."

LIES. Straight from the pit of hell. And you ought to rebuke that thought *on sight*:

> "You weren't the villain. You were the *victim*. But now you've become your own captor by carrying chains God never gave you."

Shame and unforgiveness walk hand-in-hand and you must break the partnership, by any means necessary!

3. Talk it out

Silence is where the enemy *sets up shop*. The longer you keep it in, the deeper it *roots in*.

You're not weak for needing help—you're *wise*. It takes strength to say, 'I can't carry this alone.' Even Jesus had Simon carry His cross!

Whether it's therapy, a prayer partner, or a trusted leader—talk. Get it out. Let the tears fall. Let the healing flow.

4. Rebuild with purpose

> "Forgiveness is not just letting go—it's *leaning forward*."

Depression says: "There's no reason to try." God says: *"I give you beauty for ashes."* (Isaiah 61:3)

Go back to the place where joy used to live. Serve again. Laugh again. Dream again. Don't wait to feel better— *move while it still hurts.*

"Healing comes to those who walk—*not those who wait.*"

Final Charge: Depression is real. But so is deliverance.

Let's be real. Forgiveness won't always cure clinical depression. But it *will* unclog the emotional drain that's been siphoning your soul. And for many, that's where the light starts to crack in.

You may need therapy. You may need medicine. But you *definitely* need to release that weight. Because some of you are walking around with a casket full of pain—and wondering why resurrection power won't touch you.

Let go. Not because it's easy. But because your **joy, your purpose, and your future are on the other side** of what you're still dragging.

Reflect, Release & Realign

What did this chapter reveal about your own heart?

Have you experienced this behavior or emotion in your own life? How has it affected you or others?

Who or what do you need to forgive—past or present—to break free from this?

What truth from God's Word stood out most in this chapter? How can you apply it?

What steps can you take this week to walk in forgiveness and healing?

E – Entitlement & Envy: Poisoned Perspectives

Scripture to Reflect On: Luke 15:29–30, Proverbs 14:30, Galatians 6:4

Entitlement and envy often go hand in hand, and both are fed by unforgiveness. When we feel wronged, we may begin to believe that the world owes us something. That God owes us something. That justice should've been served by now. This sense of entitlement morphs into envy when we see others receiving what we feel we've been denied.

1. Entitlement is the **silent arrogance** of the offended.

> *"Look! All these years I've been slaving for you and never disobeyed your orders..."* — Luke 15:29

That's the older brother in the story of the prodigal son—and

He wasn't holy—he was *hateful*. He didn't want his brother to come home—he wanted *repayment*. Some of y'all aren't mad because they sinned— you're mad because they got forgiven before you got *credit*.

Entitlement says, *"I deserve better."*
But the cross says, *"You deserve death—and still got grace."*

2. Unforgiveness will make you demand blessings and

despise mercy.

Entitlement grows in pain that hasn't healed and justice that hasn't happened.

> "You're not standing on a promise—you're standing on a *grudge*. And now you think God owes you something because people didn't treat you right. But newsflash: God is not your employee. He's not on your payroll."

You'll know entitlement is in the room when you:

- Constantly feeling overlooked
- Expect God to make people *pay you back*
- Can't move forward without *an apology first*
- Believe suffering qualifies you for special treatment

Stop keeping score and start keeping *faith*.
Healing doesn't need a receipt. It needs *release*.

3. Envy: The Spiritual Cancer of Comparison

> "A heart at peace gives life to the body, but envy rots the bones." — Proverbs 14:30

Envy says: *"Why not me?"*
Entitlement says: *"That should've been me!"*
And unforgiveness *fuels both*.

> "You can't celebrate anyone else because you think God forgot about you. But maybe He's trying to *fix you* before He *favors you*."

Signs that envy is sitting in your pew:

- You feel low-key tight when someone else wins

- You scroll social media and feel more discouraged than inspired

- You find it hard to clap for others

- You start questioning God's fairness

  "You say it's just disappointment. But it's *envy in disguise*. You're mad that grace is working for people you thought didn't deserve it."

Shifting the Focus: Get Out of God's Seat

1. Call it out

You can't cast out what you keep petting. Say it:

- "God, I've been bitter because they're winning and I'm waiting."

- "God, I've been acting like You owe me something."
  Confession isn't weakness—it's *warfare*.

2. Practice gratitude

You can't praise and pout at the same time. Gratitude realigns your sight.

You'll always think you're losing if you're looking at someone else's lane. But the moment you thank God for *what you already have*, you break the back of entitlement.

Start simple. Thank Him for breath. For sanity. For survival. For not letting what broke you be the end of you.

3. Forgive

At the root of entitlement is often a *robbery in your spirit*, something you felt was stolen: time, innocence, opportunity.
But forgiveness is how you tell the devil:

> "You *can't keep charging me* for what Jesus already paid for."

4. Trust God's timing

God's not late. He's just not doing it *your way*. And if you're too focused on their harvest, you'll miss your seed.

Some of y'all are mad at God for not giving you fruit—but you *haven't even planted obedience.*

Final Charge: You're Not Owed—You're *Graced*

This isn't about getting what you deserve. It's about thanking God you *didn't* get what you did deserve.

God doesn't bless on your *timeline*—He blesses based on His *glory*. Stop trying to manage His mercy.

The cure for entitlement is *humility*.
The cure for envy is *gratitude*.
And the cure for both is *forgiveness*.

You don't have to beg God.
You don't have to compete.
Just surrender. He's not withholding it—He's *preparing* you for it.

Reflect, Release & Realign

What did this chapter reveal about your own heart?

Have you experienced this behavior or emotion in your own life? How has it affected you or others?

Who or what do you need to forgive—past or present—to break free from this?

What truth from God's Word stood out most in this chapter? How can you apply it?

What steps can you take this week to walk in forgiveness and healing?

F – Fear: The Prison Guard of Unforgiveness

Scripture to Reflect On: 1 John 4:18, Isaiah 41:10

Fear is one of the most powerful weapons unforgiveness uses to keep us bound. When we've been hurt deeply, fear steps in to protect us. It says, "Never trust again," "Stay guarded," or "Don't be vulnerable." But fear doesn't protect you, if allowed, it will imprison you. It keeps us behind emotional bars, locked away from love, healing and restoration.

Fear's False Promises

Fear promises safety but delivers isolation. It convinces us that staying closed off will keep us from getting hurt again. But instead of shielding us, fear shrinks our world. We avoid meaningful relationships, sabotage new opportunities, and brace for hurt, even when none is coming.

Common fears rooted in unforgiveness:

- Fear of being hurt again
- Fear of being seen as weak
- Fear of vulnerability or intimacy
- Fear that forgiveness means losing control or power

1. Fear doesn't guard your heart, it *grips* it.

   "Perfect love casts out fear..." — 1 John 4:18
   "Do not fear, for I am with you..." — Isaiah 41:10

Let's be clear: Fear doesn't come in peace. It comes to *paralyze.*

Unforgiveness invites it in. Hurt gives it a seat. And before long, it's guarding the gates of your emotions, your trust, and your relationships.

You thought fear was your armor. Nah. It's your *warden*. And you're calling it wisdom—but God is calling it *bondage*.

2. Fear's Lies: "Protection" That Ends in Isolation

Fear whispers:

- "Don't open up. They'll just use you."

- "Don't trust. You'll get played again."

- "Don't forgive. You'll look weak."

But here's the real: **Fear makes you build walls so high that not even** *God's healing* **can reach you.**

You're not cautious—you're *captive*. And the cell door's been open the whole time... but you've been hugging the bars like they're your comfort zone.

Common Fears That Grow in the Soil of Unforgiveness:

- **Fear of being hurt again**: You brace for betrayal before love even walks in.

- **Fear of appearing weak**: You've made strength an idol. You can't even cry without apologizing.

- **Fear of vulnerability**: You call it boundaries— but it's really just fear dressed up in control.

- **Fear that forgiveness means losing power**: You think if you let go, you lose leverage. Truth is, *you're already losing joy.*

Breaking the Grip of Fear

1. Name your fear out loud

> "Fear thrives in the shadows. Drag it into the light and watch it start to *choke.*"

Say it:

- "I'm scared to trust again."
- "I'm afraid of being abandoned."
- "I don't want to be vulnerable."

Naming it doesn't make you weak—it makes you *dangerous to the devil.*

2. Challenge the narrative

Is it fear or is it fiction?

Some of y'all are running from a pain that's not even chasing you anymore. You're still defending yourself from ghosts.

The mind doesn't know the difference between memory and threat until you tell it: *"This is not 1986. This is not the divorce. This is not the betrayal. This is now—and I am no longer bound."*

3. Step forward *even while afraid*

Courage isn't waiting until you're unafraid. Courage is shaking, sweating, weeping—and *still stepping*!

Start small. Say "yes" to the new friendship. Open up a little. Trust God with one more piece of your heart.

Every act of forgiveness is a **rebellion against fear**.

4. Lean into God's perfect love

1 John 4:18 doesn't say love *negotiates* with fear. It says it **casts it out**—*violently.*

> "When you soak in God's love, you don't have to build walls. His love becomes your *refuge*. Not your pain. Not your past. *Him*."

You were never meant to be guarded by trauma—you were meant to be *kept* by grace.

Final Charge: Forgiveness Breaks Fear's Grip—But Only If You Move

Fear won't move until you *push it*.
Fear won't break until you *step past it*.
And you can't step forward while hugging the pain of your past.

God didn't give you the spirit of fear. But you *adopted it* when you refused to heal. Now it sleeps in your bed, rides in your car, and sits in your prayers. But today—it's got to *go*.

This isn't just about feeling better. It's about being *free*.

Forgive.
Face it.
Move anyway.
And let God's love become your shield.

Reflect, Release & Realign

What did this chapter reveal about your own heart?

Have you experienced this behavior or emotion in your own life? How has it affected you or others?

Who or what do you need to forgive—past or present—to break free from this?

What truth from God's Word stood out most in this chapter? How can you apply it?

What steps can you take this week to walk in forgiveness and healing?

G – Grudges: The Chains You Choose to Wear

Scripture to Reflect On: Leviticus 19:18, Mark 11:25

A grudge is unforgiveness in long-term storage. It's the refusal to let go, the quiet vow that says, "I'll never forget what you did." Holding a grudge feels like power, like you're taking control back—but in reality, it's a chain that binds you to the pain of the past.

The Burden That Gets Heavier Over Time

Grudges grow heavier the longer you carry them. What started as a justified offense slowly becomes a lifestyle of resentment. You may no longer remember the full story, just that you're still angry. And worse, the person you're holding the grudge against may be oblivious, living freely while you're still bound.

Signs you're carrying a grudge:

- Replaying the offense in your mind regularly
- Avoiding or resenting the person involved
- Talking about the pain more than the healing
- Secret satisfaction when the other person suffers or struggles

1. A grudge is not strength—it's *slavery.*

> *"Do not seek revenge or bear a grudge... but love your neighbor as yourself."* — Leviticus 19:18
> *"And when you stand praying, forgive..."* — Mark 11:25

Please understand that grudges are not trophies. They're *chains.* You keep flexing your pain like it's a badge of honor. And if you're so free, then why are you still *bound* to that name? That moment? That pain? These are the questions that you should ask yourself.

You're not holding a grudge. *It's holding you.*

2. Grudges are pain that made a permanent address.

At first, it was real. You were hurt. Disrespected. Violated.
But instead of healing, you *hardened*.
And now, the pain moved from your *memory* into your *personality*.

Some of y'all forgot the full story—but you remember the grudge. You remember the betrayal more than the blessing. And now, you *live to rehearse the hurt.*

And the worst part?

They moved on. You didn't.
They're eating. Sleeping. Loving.
Meanwhile, *you're chained to yesterday*. And every time you smile, the enemy yanks the chain.

Signs You're Carrying a Grudge

- **Replaying the offense**: If the pain still plays in HD every night, you're not healed.

- **Avoidance or tension**: If their presence still shifts your posture—you're not free.

- **Talking more about the pain than the healing**: If the hurt has more airtime than your healing—you're feeding it.

- **Secretly celebrating their struggles**: If their downfall feels like justice... you're bitter with a bow on it.

Don't tell me you forgave them when you get joy watching them fail. That's not peace—that's a petty spirit.

Letting Go Without Losing Yourself

1. Understand what you're really carrying

It's not just an offense. It's a mindset.
You've become suspicious, cynical, and emotionally fatigued—and you call it *discernment*.

> "Grudges disguise themselves as wisdom. But really, it's just *woundedness with vocabulary*."

Ask yourself: *Is this pain helping me heal or holding me hostage?*

2. Separate identity from offense

You are *not* what they did to you.
You are *not* the moment they let you down.
You are not the affair. Not the betrayal. Not the abandonment.
You are who *God called you—even with the scar.*

> "Stop letting the offense name you. Only the One who formed you has the right to define you."

3. Release the need for justice

You're not the judge—you're the *healed*. You're not the jury, you're the *delivered*. You're not God—so stop trying to manage vengeance with your flesh.

Let God deal with them. You deal with *your freedom*.

4. Take action to move forward

Don't wait for a feeling—make a *faith move*:

- Write the letter and burn it.
- Say the name out loud and release them in prayer.
- If it's safe, talk it out.
- If it's not, talk to God *about* it until your soul gets lighter.

Declare:

"Today, I choose peace over pain."

And if you've got to say that for 30 days straight until the chains fall off—then so be it. *Freedom is worth the fight.*

Final Charge: You're Wearing Chains You Were Never Meant to Own

From me to you:

"Grudges don't keep you strong. They keep you stuck. You think you're punishing them, but you're sentencing *yourself*—to stagnation, to silence, to spiritual suffocation."

You hold the key.
You control the weight.
You can live *unchained*.

Forgive.
Break free.
And stop building your future from the materials of your offense.

Reflect, Release & Realign

What did this chapter reveal about your own heart?

Have you experienced this behavior or emotion in your own life? How has it affected you or others?

Who or what do you need to forgive—past or present—to break free from this?

What truth from God's Word stood out most in this chapter? How can you apply it?

What steps can you take this week to walk in forgiveness and healing?

H – Hatred: The Poison That Consumes the Heart

Scripture to Reflect On: 1 John 2:9–11, Proverbs 10:12

Hatred is the final stage of unchecked hurt. When unforgiveness simmers long enough, it transforms into hate—a deep-rooted hostility that craves harm rather than healing. Hatred is never born overnight. It is brewed in betrayal, stirred by bitterness, and fed by a refusal to forgive.

The Soul-Destroying Force of Hatred

Hatred isn't always loud. Sometimes, it's a quiet seething. A deep chill when their name is mentioned. A hardened smile when they stumble. But make no mistake—hatred is lethal. It deforms your character, damages your witness, and deadens your spirit. You can't hate someone without it costing you a piece of yourself.

How hatred manifests:

- Wishing the worst on someone who hurt you
- Speaking ill of them regularly
- Celebrating their failures
- Losing compassion for others entirely

1. Hatred is what happens when your wound becomes your worldview.

> *"Anyone who hates a brother or sister is in the darkness..."* — 1 John 2:11

"Hatred stirs up conflict, but love covers all wrongs." — Proverbs 10:12

Hatred doesn't show up with horns and fire—it slides in through *hurt you refused to heal.* You didn't wake up hateful...you *fed it* with offense, day by day.

You thought you were guarding your heart. Nah— **you've been poisoning it.**
And here's the catch: *You don't even feel it anymore.* Because hatred numbs before it kills.

2. Hate doesn't hide—it leaks.

You may not curse them out or slash their tires. But:

- That smirk when they fall?
- That satisfaction when they're exposed?
- That story you told about them...again?

You're not healed. You're *hollow.* You don't walk in love. You *limp in hate.* And the devil is banking on you not calling it out.

You cannot claim to love God and *harbor hell* in your heart.

How Hatred Manifests:
- Wishing someone would "get what they deserve"
- Constantly running them down in conversation
- Relishing in their failures
- Losing love for people in general because of one person in particular

You think you're justified—but you're actually *judged*.
Not by them. By the condition of your own soul."

Choosing Healing Over Hate

1. Recognize hatred for what it is

It's not "just anger." It's not "just keeping your distance."
It's *sin*.
And *it stinks in the nostrils of God*.

Don't spiritualize your hate by calling it 'righteous indignation.' There's nothing holy about *hardened hearts*.

2. Remember your own need for mercy

You didn't get everything you deserved either. So why weaponize grace when it's your turn to extend it?

You're not the hero in every story. Sometimes you were the villain. And God still forgave *you*.

3. Pray for them—on purpose

> "You're not ready for healing until you can bless the one who broke you."

Pray not in sarcasm, but in *sincerity*.
Because when you pray for them—God begins to *repair you*.

4. Displace hatred with love

Love doesn't mean you re-enter a toxic relationship. It means you *exit the prison of pain*.

You don't have to like them. But you *do* have to release them. Love is how you take the hand off your neck—and put it into God's hands.

Final Charge: Hatred doesn't make you powerful—it makes you pitiful.

It's not hurting them—it's *eating you alive.*
You want vengeance. God wants *victory.*
You want justice. God wants *joy.*
You want pain. God wants to give you *peace.*

Let it go.
Forgive.
Get free.

Reflect, Release & Realign

What did this chapter reveal about your own heart?

Have you experienced this behavior or emotion in your own life? How has it affected you or others?

Who or what do you need to forgive—past or present—to break free from this?

What truth from God's Word stood out most in this chapter? How can you apply it?

What steps can you take this week to walk in forgiveness and healing?

I – Isolation: The Lonely Road of Unforgiveness

Scripture to Reflect On: Ecclesiastes 4:9–10, Hebrews 10:25

Unforgiveness doesn't just affect how you feel, it shapes how you live. One of its most damaging side effects is isolation. When we've been wounded and choose not to forgive, we start building emotional walls. We tell ourselves it's for protection, but those same walls that keep pain out also keep love and connection away.

When Self-Protection Becomes Self-Imprisonment

You withdraw not just from the one who hurt you, but from everyone. You stop trusting. You stop opening up. You convince yourself you're better off alone, but deep inside, loneliness grows like a shadow. Isolation might feel safe, but it's not healing. It's surviving, not living.

Signs of isolation rooted in unforgiveness:

- Pulling away from relationships, even healthy ones
- Refusing to share emotions or personal struggles
- Feeling misunderstood or unloved
- Using busyness or distractions to avoid vulnerability

1. You don't just shut people out—you shut *healing* out.

> *"Woe to the one who falls and has no one to help them up."* — Ecclesiastes 4:10

Some of y'all are not introverts. You're *injured.*

And now you're hiding your wound in the name of wisdom—but it's really *withered trust.*

Isolation may feel safe. But it's a slow death.

2. Self-protection becomes self-imprisonment when fear wears the crown.

You built a wall to keep pain out.
But that same wall is keeping *purpose, love,* and *support* from getting in.

You weren't created for caves. You were built for *connection.* But unforgiveness told you, 'Don't trust again.' Now you're alive... but not *living.*

Signs You're in the Isolation Trap:

- Pulling back from healthy relationships
- Hiding your emotions under busyness
- Feeling invisible or misunderstood
- Refusing to ask for help even when you're drowning

And worst of all?

> "You've made loneliness your new *language.* You speak 'I'm fine'—but your spirit is *screaming for rescue.*"

Finding Freedom Through Reconnection

1. Acknowledge the fear behind your walls

It's not strength—it's *shielding.*

- Fear of being hurt again
- Fear of exposure

- Fear of being too much or not enough

Name it. Shame it. Then *slay it*. Fear exposed is fear *dismantled*.

2. Give yourself permission to heal in community

God never designed you to *heal in hiding*. Deliverance comes through *connection*—iron sharpening iron, love confronting wounds, community breaking cycles.

You don't need a stage. You need a *circle*. One person you can tell the truth to, can change your whole life.

3. Rebuild trust gradually

Start small:

- One vulnerable conversation
- One prayer partner
- One step toward being *seen* again

Every act of vulnerability is a brick toward *restoration*.

4. Invite God into your solitude

Even in your aloneness—you're *not abandoned*.

> "God's not just waiting at the altar. He's sitting in the *darkness* with you. And He'll stay until you're ready to *walk out*."

Final Charge: Isolation lies. Forgiveness liberates.

Unforgiveness told you:

> "Stay hidden. Stay guarded. Stay distant."

But God is calling you:

"Come out. Come closer. Come *home*."

You don't have to be the strong one anymore.
You just have to be the *healing* one.

Reflect, Release & Realign

What did this chapter reveal about your own heart?

Have you experienced this behavior or emotion in your own life? How has it affected you or others?

Who or what do you need to forgive—past or present—to break free from this?

What truth from God's Word stood out most in this chapter? How can you apply it?

What steps can you take this week to walk in forgiveness and healing?

J – Jealousy & Judgmental Spirit: The Twin Thieves of Joy

Scripture to Reflect On: Romans 12:15, Matthew 7:1–5

When unforgiveness goes unchecked, it gives birth to two subtle yet destructive attitudes: jealousy and a judgmental spirit. These twin thieves don't just steal your peace—they poison how you see others and how you see yourself. While one whispers, "Why not me?" the other declares, "I'd never be like them." Both are rooted in unresolved pain, and both will block your path to healing.

The Corruption of Comparison

Jealousy creeps in when you see the person who hurt you thriving while you're still struggling. It doesn't seem fair. You think, *"They should be suffering and not succeeding!"* Resentment grows when their joy triggers your pain. And instead of healing, you rehearse the injustice.

A judgmental spirit is often pride disguised as righteousness. You elevate your morality over the offender's flaws. It feels safe to stand on the high ground, but it's a lonely, cold place. When you judge harshly, you build a wall between yourself and grace.

Signs of jealousy and a judgmental spirit:

- Secret envy when others succeed, especially the one who hurt you

- Harsh inner dialogue or public criticism of others' faults

- Difficulty celebrating others' victories

- A growing sense of superiority or spiritual pride

1. Jealousy and judgment don't show up dressed in evil—they show up dressed in **ego**.

> *"Rejoice with those who rejoice..."* — Romans 12:15
> *"Why do you look at the speck in your brother's eye..."* — Matthew 7:3

Jealousy says: "They didn't deserve that."
Judgment says: "I would've never done that."

You're not envious because they got it, you're envious because you're *not healed yet*. You're not judgmental because you're holy—you're judgmental because you're *hurting and hiding it in spiritual language*.

2. You can't hold onto jealousy and judgment and expect joy to stay.

They don't just rob your peace—they **infect your lens**. You can't even see others' success without tasting bitterness in your mouth. And instead of addressing the broken mirror in your soul—you start smashing others to feel whole.

Jealousy and judgment are the *twins of trauma*. They were born out of betrayal, but raised by your refusal to forgive.

How They Show Up:
- **You flinch when others win**
- **You get quiet when others get promoted**

- **You correct but never cover**
- **You criticize what you secretly crave**

It matters not who you are or what your title is, you can't be more anointed online than you are in your *attitude*. Don't ever be found posting about grace, but pray for people to fall. That is not holiness—that's *hypocrisy*."

How to Uproot the Twins of Torment

1. Face your wounds honestly

> "The loudest judges are usually the ones bleeding the most silently."

Look inward:

- What did they get that you feel you should've?
- Who did they forgive that you still haven't?

This isn't about them. It's about *you finally getting healed.*

2. Celebrate others on purpose

Start clapping even when it hurts. Send the compliment. Bless them in public and private. And *watch God do open-heart surgery on your soul.*

Gratitude will choke jealousy to death. Try it.

3. Remember your own grace story

You've messed up too. And *you got away with some stuff nobody but God knows about.*

You can't be a recipient of mercy and a dispenser of judgment at the same time.

4. Let God be the Judge

Take the gavel off your lap. Let it go. Judgment is too heavy for your hands.

Final Charge: Stop policing everyone else's life while your soul is bleeding out.

Jealousy is poison. Judgment is pride. And both are BLOCKING your blessing.

Forgiveness isn't just about what they did—it's about what you're *still carrying*. Let it go before it kills you from the inside out.

Reflect, Release & Realign

What did this chapter reveal about your own heart?

Have you experienced this behavior or emotion in your own life? How has it affected you or others?

Who or what do you need to forgive—past or present—to break free from this?

What truth from God's Word stood out most in this chapter? How can you apply it?

What steps can you take this week to walk in forgiveness and healing?

K – Keeping Score: The Ledger That Never Lets You Live

Scripture to Reflect On: 1 Corinthians 13:5, Psalm 32:1

Unforgiveness thrives on memory, but not the kind that brings wisdom. It thrives on the kind that keeps score. Every offense recorded. Every slight cataloged. Every wound logged. Keeping score feels like staying in control, but in reality, it traps you in a cycle of reliving pain. You can't move forward while your heart is stuck in the past.

The Illusion of Control

When we keep score, we believe we're protecting ourselves. We think, *If I remember what they did, I'll never get hurt like that again.* But all we're doing is building a case for bitterness. And over time, that case becomes a courtroom where we become judge, jury, and emotional prisoner.

The cost of keeping score:

- Emotional exhaustion from constantly reliving the past

- Distrust in future relationships

- Overreactions to small triggers because of stored resentment

- A heart too full of old offenses to receive new joy

1. You're not remembering—you're *recording.*

> *"Love keeps no record of wrongs..."* — 1 Corinthians 13:5
> *"Blessed is the one whose sin the Lord does*

not count against them." — Psalm 32:1

If I'm being honest, I believe that some of people are not walking in love—they're running a courtroom in their mind. You've got timestamps, screenshots and mental spreadsheets and receipts. And guess what? *You're the prisoner, not the judge.*

2. Keeping score doesn't protect you—it **poisons** you.

Every replay is a re-injury.
Every mental note is a *nail in your own freedom.*
And that tally you keep? It's not holding *them* accountable—it's holding *you* hostage.

Your spirit is cluttered with past offenses, and you wonder why there's no room for new joy. You can't receive tomorrow's blessing while clenching yesterday's bitterness.

Signs You're a Scorekeeper:

- Constantly replaying conversations

- Keeping emotional receipts

- Judging every current interaction through old offenses

- Using sarcasm as a shield but seething underneath

You call it 'guarding your heart'—but you're just building a museum of pain. And you keep giving free tours.

Erasing the Offense Ledger

1. Recognize the habit

You're not just reminiscing—you're *reliving.* Notice

how often your peace is interrupted by someone who isn't even in the room anymore.

You say you've forgiven, but you've got a *whole spreadsheet of sins*. That is not grace—that's spiritual hoarding.

2. Decide who you want to be

You want to be healed or do you want to be *right*? You want to be whole or do you want to win arguments in your head all day?"

You can't be free and bitter. Choose.

3. Tear up the ledger

Write it. Burn it. Shred it.
Whatever you do—*destroy the evidence that keeps your soul imprisoned.*

Declare:

> "I don't need this record anymore. I need *restoration*."

4. Embrace grace, not grudges

What you release—*God replaces.*
And where grace grows—*joy flows.*

Final Charge: Let the records go. They're robbing you.

God doesn't remind you of what you did. So why do you keep a highlight reel of what *they* did?

Do you want freedom? Rip the receipt. Burn the ledger. Forgive. And live again.

Reflect, Release & Realign

What did this chapter reveal about your own heart?

Have you experienced this behavior or emotion in your own life? How has it affected you or others?

Who or what do you need to forgive—past or present—to break free from this?

What truth from God's Word stood out most in this chapter? How can you apply it?

What steps can you take this week to walk in forgiveness and healing?

L – Loss & Loneliness: The High Price of Holding On

Scripture to Reflect On: Psalm 147:3, Deuteronomy 31:6

Unforgiveness doesn't just affect how you feel, it also affects what you forfeit. When you hold onto pain, you don't just cling to the past. You also lose your present. Opportunities pass. Relationships decay. Time slips by. And when you're in your quiet time, the loneliness creeps in.

1. Unforgiveness doesn't just cost you peace—it costs you **pieces** of your life.

> *"He heals the brokenhearted and binds up their wounds."* — Psalm 147:3
> *"He will never leave you nor forsake you."* — Deuteronomy 31:6

You thought unforgiveness only affected your *mood*. No—it hijacked your *moments*. You didn't just lose them—you started *losing you*. Your joy. Your softness. Your openness. And now, you're just a ghost walking through what used to be your life.

2. Loss isn't just what was taken—it's what **you stopped receiving**.

Unforgiveness shuts the windows of your soul. And while you're focused on what left, you don't even realize what's been blocked:

- Love
- Peace

- Purpose
- People

Some of y'all are so focused on who hurt you, that you missed who God *sent to heal you*. You lost *time* chasing *vengeance* when God was offering *restoration*.

Common Losses Tied to Unforgiveness:

- **Loss of emotional intimacy**
- **Loss of trust in good people**
- **Loss of years stuck in resentment**
- **Loss of purpose because of paralyzed vision**

You can't walk into your future when your eyes are glued to the rearview mirror.

The Loneliness That Lingers:

You can be surrounded by people... and still be alone.
You laugh—but it's hollow.
You smile—but it's guarded.
Why? Because you've been *wounded and walled off*.

Unforgiveness convinces you that isolation is safety. But that's not safety—it's *solitary confinement for the soul*.

Choosing Restoration Over Regret

1. Grieve the real losses

Don't downplay it. Don't bury it. *Name it*. You can't heal from what you won't mourn.

That friendship? That time? That version of yourself

before the betrayal? Mourn it. Then *move forward*.

2. Rebuild what can be rebuilt

Not everything is beyond redemption.
Some relationships are waiting for *your humility to show up before healing does*.

Don't let your pride bury something God could resurrect.

3. Let love back in

Start small. Reopen the door to connection.
It's not weakness—it's *wisdom*. It's *warfare*.

You don't need everyone—but you do need *someone*. Don't die in a room full of people because you never opened your mouth.

4. Trust God with what you lost

God specializes in *resurrections*.

He can restore years. Rebuild what you buried. Rebirth what you gave up on.

Let Him. Your losses may be real, but your future is still redeemable.

Final Charge: Loss happens. But staying stuck in it is a ***choice***.

Unforgiveness stole enough already. Don't let it *own the deed* to your destiny.

Grieve it. Bury it. But don't let it bury *you*. There's still life left. Let go and go *get it*.

Reflect, Release & Realign

What did this chapter reveal about your own heart?

Have you experienced this behavior or emotion in your own life? How has it affected you or others?

Who or what do you need to forgive—past or present—to break free from this?

What truth from God's Word stood out most in this chapter? How can you apply it?

What steps can you take this week to walk in forgiveness and healing?

M – Misery: The Emotional Prison of Unforgiveness

Scripture to Reflect On: Lamentations 3:19-23, Proverbs 15:13

Misery is what happens when you marinate in unresolved pain. You're not just dealing with sadness, it's sustained sorrow, the kind that darkens your days and drags down your spirit. Misery tells you nothing will ever change, and it thrives when unforgiveness is left unchecked.

When Pain Becomes Your Atmosphere

Misery isn't always loud. Sometimes it's quiet despair. A heaviness that follows you. A constant emotional fatigue. Unforgiveness keeps misery alive by chaining you to the offense, making sure you never truly move forward, even if everything around you does.

1. Misery is the child of memory without mercy.

> *"I well remember them, and my soul is downcast within me. Yet this I call to mind... great is Your faithfulness."* — Lamentations 3:19–23
> *"A joyful heart makes a cheerful face, but when the heart is sad, the spirit is broken."* — Proverbs 15:13

Misery isn't just depression—it's *devotion to your pain.* It's the altar you built to the offense. You light candles of memory and call it 'processing.'

But what you're really doing... is *worshipping your wounds.*

2. Unforgiveness is the air misery breathes.

You don't need more sleep. You need *release.*
You don't need more distractions. You need *deliverance.*

You're not lazy—you're *leaking.*
You're not numb—you're *suffocating from suppressed sorrow.*

How Misery Shows Up:

- Apathy toward life
- Numbness to joy
- Fatigue that sleep can't fix
- Constant loop of "what they did" playing in your mind

You can't fake freedom when your soul is fatigued.
Misery will make you look alive but feel *empty.*

How to Escape the Pit of Misery

1. Name the misery without shame

Say it:

- "I'm not okay."
- "I'm still hurt."
- "I'm tired of being tired."

Freedom always starts with *confession*, not pretending.

2. Interrupt the pattern

Misery loves cycles:

- Overthinking
- Regret
- Self-pity
- Silent suffering

Break the loop. Open your mouth. Dance when you feel like dying. Worship when you feel worn. Shake the foundation.

3. Forgive forward

Don't wait until you *feel* like forgiving. Start walking even while you're weeping!

Forgiveness shrinks the power of the past and *amplifies the potential of the present.*

4. Pursue joy on purpose

Joy is not a mood—it's a *mission.*

Laugh out loud even if it cracks through tears. Dream again even if it feels foolish. That's not denial—it's *deliverance in motion.*

Final Charge: Misery is a prison in which you don't belong.

You've camped out at sorrow's address long enough. Now it's time to *forward your mail.*

Unforgiveness built the cell, but *forgiveness holds the key.* Walk out. Wipe your face. And get back to living.

Reflect, Release & Realign

What did this chapter reveal about your own heart?

Have you experienced this behavior or emotion in your own life? How has it affected you or others?

Who or what do you need to forgive—past or present—to break free from this?

What truth from God's Word stood out most in this chapter? How can you apply it?

What steps can you take this week to walk in forgiveness and healing?

N – Negative Mindset & Numbness: When Pain Rewrites Your Perspective

Scripture to Reflect On: Philippians 4:8, Ezekiel 36:26

I'm sure you know, but in case you don't, know that unforgiveness doesn't just affect your heart—it rewires your mind. It shifts how you interpret the world around you. The longer you hold onto offense, the more your thoughts default to suspicion, pessimism, and defeat. This is the birth of a negative mindset. But right beside it often comes its cousin: numbness. When pain is too heavy for too long, the heart stops feeling altogether. You go from overthinking to underfeeling—and neither of the two are freedom.

1. Unforgiveness doesn't just live in your heart, moves into your head, and changes the locks.

> *"Think on these things..."* — Philippians 4:8
> *"I will give you a new heart and put a new spirit in you..."* — Ezekiel 36:26

Some of y'all don't even realize—your thinking has been hijacked. Pain has become your narrator. Offense has become your filter. And now you can't tell the difference between discernment and dysfunction.

2. Negativity is not your personality—it's your prison.

When you live in unforgiveness long enough:

- A compliment feels fake.
- A kind gesture feels suspicious.

- Hope feels foolish.

Why? Because pain is holding the microphone, and it never stops preaching:
"They'll hurt you again. Nobody can be trusted. Joy won't last."

That's not the Holy Ghost talking—that's your history talking. And until you change the voice you're listening to, you'll keep living in the same chapter while the book of your life moves on without you.

3. Numbness is not peace—it's paralysis.

When pain gets too heavy, numbness moves in. And here's the dangerous part—it doesn't just block pain, it blocks:

- Joy

- Love

- God's presence

You're alive but you're not *living*. You've got a heartbeat but no *holy fire*.

You think you're safe because you can't feel hurt anymore, but you've also lost your ability to feel God. That's not protection—that's spiritual frostbite.

Signs the Cycle Has Taken Over:

Negative Mindset:

- Always expecting the worst

- Distrusting good moments

- Talking about what broke you more than what's

building you

- Speaking doubt instead of destiny

Numbness:

- Emotionally checked out
- No excitement for growth or change
- Inability to cry or celebrate
- Living distracted to avoid dealing with the truth

How to Rewire & Reawaken

1. Capture every thought

2 Corinthians 10:5 says to take every thought captive—because if you don't, it will *take you* captive.
Ask: *"Is this thought true? Or is this my trauma talking?"*

2. Speak life until you believe it

Your heart will follow your mouth.
Declare:

> "I am healing. I am forgiving. I will feel again.
> I will love again."

3. Lean into safe spaces

Isolation feeds numbness. Reconnection starves it.
Spend time with people who actually love you—let their presence thaw your heart.

4. Give yourself grace to feel again

This is not instant coffee—it's a slow simmer. Let God reawaken you one tear, one laugh, one prayer at a time.

Final Charge:

Negative thinking will drain your hope.
Numbness will drain your humanity.
Unforgiveness will keep you stuck in *both*.

If the enemy can control your thoughts, he'll
control your future. But if God renews your mind,
He'll resurrect your life. You can get your fire
back. You can get your faith back. But you can't
keep unforgiveness and expect to think—or feel—
like the healed.

Reflect, Release & Realign

What did this chapter reveal about your own heart?

Have you experienced this behavior or emotion in your own life? How has it affected you or others?

Who or what do you need to forgive—past or present—to break free from this?

What truth from God's Word stood out most in this chapter? How can you apply it?

What steps can you take this week to walk in forgiveness and healing?

O – Offense: The Open Door to Division

Scripture to Reflect On: Proverbs 19:11, Luke 17:3–4

Offense is the bait of unforgiveness. It draws you in with a sense of justice but entraps you in a cycle of emotional instability and separation. When you live offended, you give power to every slight, real or perceived. And once offense settles in, it will begin to build walls—between friends, within families and even between you and God.

1. Offense is the bait. Division is the trap.

> *"It is to one's glory to overlook an offense."*
> — Proverbs 19:11
> *"If your brother sins against you, rebuke him; and if he repents, forgive him."* — Luke 17:3

The enemy doesn't need to destroy you—he just needs to *offend* you. Because if he can get you in your feelings, he can get you out of your faith.

Offense always *feels* like protection. But the truth? It's **possession**—a slow spiritual takeover.

2. Offense turns wounds into identity.

At first, you were *hurt.*
Then you became *offended.*
Now, offense has *become who you are.*

You've moved from:

- Experiencing pain → to *embracing* pain → to *embodying* pain.

Some of y'all don't even need a reason to be mad anymore—you've trained yourself to find one. That's not discernment—that's dysfunction in disguise.

3. The Slow Poison of Offense

Signs You're Living in Offense:

- Feeling attacked by feedback
- Overreacting to small slights
- Always replaying what they did or didn't do
- Cutting people off instead of confronting with love

And the worst part?
Offense doesn't just divide you from people—it will quietly **distance you from God**.

You'll start singing less, serving less, showing up less—not because you don't love God, but because you got stuck on something *someone* did.

How to Live Unoffended

1. Choose not to personalize everything

Some people aren't cruel, they're just careless. Some don't mean to hurt you—they're just broken themselves.

Not everything is an attack. Sometimes it's just life.

2. Respond with grace, not retaliation

Offense wants you to *clap back*. Grace wants you to *step back*.

You can't heal acting like them—you heal by reflecting Him.

3. Practice spiritual maturity

Immaturity keeps offense like a pet. Maturity says, *"This can't stay in my house."*

Use offense as a **mirror**, not a **mask**—let it reveal what's still unhealed.

4. Anchor your identity in Christ

If you know who you are, you don't need an apology to move on.
If your value is in Jesus, they can't bankrupt your peace.

Final Charge:

Offense is an *entry point* for the enemy. And every day you hold it, you're basically paying rent for hell to live in your heart.

You can't live unoffended without living forgiven.
So, either you close the door today—or watch offense open it wider tomorrow. Your choice.

Reflect, Release & Realign

What did this chapter reveal about your own heart?

Have you experienced this behavior or emotion in your own life? How has it affected you or others?

Who or what do you need to forgive—past or present—to break free from this?

What truth from God's Word stood out most in this chapter? How can you apply it?

What steps can you take this week to walk in forgiveness and healing?

P – Pride, Punishment & Poison: The Triple Threat That Blocks Healing

Scripture to Reflect On: Proverbs 16:18, Romans 12:19, James 3:8–10

Unforgiveness gives rise to three dangerous forces—pride, punishment, and poison. Pride whispers, *"You're better than them. You don't need to forgive."* Punishment hisses, *"Make them feel what you felt."* Poison silently spreads, infecting your emotions, decisions, and destiny. These are not just responses to pain—they are barriers to peace. Each one convinces you you're protecting yourself, but together, they keep you bound.

1. Unforgiveness is not just an emotion, it's an ecosystem.

> *"Pride goes before destruction..."* — Proverbs 16:18
> *"Do not take revenge... leave room for God's wrath."* — Romans 12:19
> *"The tongue is a restless evil, full of deadly poison."* — James 3:8

You thought you were just mad. You thought you were just hurt. But the devil saw an opening—and now you're walking around infected with *three silent killers*: pride, punishment, and poison.

These three don't walk alone—they travel together, whispering lies, wrapping chains, and blocking every ounce of the healing God has for you.

PRIDE: The Wall That Blocks Healing

Pride says:

- "I don't need to deal with this."
- "They're wrong. I'm right."
- "I'd never do what they did."

But here is the stone-cold truth:

> "You can't be *healed and hardened*. You can't be *restored and rehearsing the wrongs*. Pride builds walls so thick not even grace can break through—*until you humble yourself first*."

Signs of Pride in Unforgiveness:

- Avoiding vulnerability
- Refusing to acknowledge your flaws in the fallout
- Calling forgiveness "weakness"
- Needing to look "strong" even while bleeding inside

PUNISHMENT: The Illusion of Justice

You say you're done, but you're *strategically withdrawing*. You're *snubbing with intent*. You've weaponized silence and camouflaged cruelty as boundaries.

You're not holding them accountable—you're holding yourself *hostage*. You can't be the warden and the one in chains.

Signs of a Punishment Mindset:

- Secretly hoping they suffer

- Repeating the story to demonize them
- Holding love hostage until they meet your expectations
- Making your healing *conditional* on their behavior

POISON: The Silent Contaminant

This is the most dangerous of the three. You don't even realize it's leaking:

- Into new relationships
- Into your worship
- Into your words
- Into your own *self-worth*

And the scary part? You'll think you're protecting yourself while you're actually **contaminating everyone and everything around you.**

You're bitter at people who never touched you. Suspicious of love that was pure. Guarded from God when all He wanted to do was heal. That's not protection. That's *toxic residue from a grudge that should've been buried years ago.*

Signs of Poison:

- Reacting too hard to trivial things
- Feeling spiritually stuck
- Withholding love from innocent people
- Losing passion for your assignment

The Path to Peace (and Power)

1. Lay down the need to be right

Being right doesn't make you free. Being *real* does.

Pride lives off superiority—healing flows from humility. Choose freedom over ego.

2. Release the need for revenge

You're not the judge. That gavel is too heavy for human hands.

Let God handle the justice. You handle the *peace*.

3. Choose vulnerability over defense

Say it:

> "I'm hurt. But I'm choosing love. I'm choosing freedom."

It takes more strength to forgive than to fight.

4. Purge the poison with grace

Grace doesn't make any excuses. It *detoxes*.
Start speaking, thinking, and acting from a healed place—not a haunted one.

5. Embrace grace—for them and for **you**

You've failed too. You've wounded too.
So stop being the end of the grace line.

You're not a reservoir—you're supposed to be a *river*.

Final Charge:

Pride will keep you bitter.
Punishment will keep you bound.
Poison will keep you broken.

Forgiveness is not surrender—it's survival.
You think unforgiveness is power—but it's just pain wearing perfume. Rip the mask off. Let pride fall. Let revenge go. Let healing begin.

It's time to *break the triple threat* and take your life back.

Reflect, Release & Realign

What did this chapter reveal about your own heart?

Have you experienced this behavior or emotion in your own life? How has it affected you or others?

Who or what do you need to forgive—past or present—to break free from this?

What truth from God's Word stood out most in this chapter? How can you apply it?

What steps can you take this week to walk in forgiveness and healing?

Q – Quitting, Quarrelsome & Quiet Resentment: The Triple Sabotage of Stunted Forgiveness

Scripture to Reflect On: Galatians 6:9, Proverbs 20:3, Ephesians 4:26

When unforgiveness lingers, it often manifests in three subtle but soul-sabotaging behaviors: quitting on people, becoming quarrelsome, and harboring quiet resentment. These responses may look different on the surface, but at their root, they are all symptoms of unhealed pain. Together, they sever relationships, silence trust, and suffocate peace.

1. Unforgiveness doesn't just hurt you—it *reprograms you*.

> *"Let us not become weary in doing good..."*
> — Galatians 6:9
> *"It is to one's honor to avoid strife..."* —
> Proverbs 20:3
> *"Do not let the sun go down while you are still angry..."* — Ephesians 4:26

You didn't used to be this short-tempered. You didn't used to be this guarded. You didn't use to leave people this fast. But unforgiveness came in and *rewrote your personality*—and now you call it 'just how I am.' That's not who you are. That's who your *hurt* has become.

2. The Triple Sabotage of Unforgiveness

Quitting on People: When Grace Runs Dry

You cut people off before God finishes the story.
You walk away instead of working it out.
You call it "protecting your peace"—but it's really
premature disconnection.

Signs:

- Silent withdrawal or ghosting

- Avoiding hard conversations

- Believing reconciliation is a waste of time

- Ending whole relationships over one moment

You think you're winning by walking away, but
you're losing what God wanted to *redeem.* Some
of y'all have a graveyard of friendships, marriages,
and connections because you buried them alive
under your unforgiveness.

Quarrelsome: Fighting Everyone Because of One

Unhealed pain makes you reactive, sharp, and
suspicious. Suddenly, every disagreement is *warfare.*
You're not even mad at **them**—you're still bleeding
from *that.*

Signs:

- Constant defensiveness

- Picking fights over small issues

- Seeing enemies where there are none

- Caring more about "winning" than about *peace*

You're shadowboxing the past while swinging on

your present. Every room feels like a battlefield because you carried yesterday's fight into today's conversation.

Quiet Resentment: The Smile That Hides the Storm

Not all unforgiveness is loud.
Sometimes it simmers like a slow leak in the soul. You smile. You nod. But underneath? You're calculating and collecting.

Signs:

- Saying "I'm fine" but staying cold inside

- Passive-aggressive comments or sarcastic jabs

- Secretly hoping they "get what's coming" without you ever having to say it

- Keeping mental score while pretending to have peace

Quiet resentment is termite damage to the soul. The house looks fine on the outside, but the foundation is *rotting*. And sooner or later—collapse is coming.

Restoring What's Been Damaged

1. Be honest about your patterns

Stop justifying them. Stop blaming everyone else. Call it what it is.

You can't heal what you keep *renaming as personality*.

2. Name the root

Follow the trail of your reactions back to the first offense that created them.

You're not mad at this moment—you're mad at that memory.

3. Make space for redemption

Not every relationship will return—but some could if you stop quitting too fast.

4. Confront with courage and compassion

Mature people don't ghost—they *grace*. They speak the truth in love and give God a chance to mend what hell tried to destroy.

5. Choose peace over pride

Whether you need to re-engage, release, or reconcile—your peace depends on your forgiveness, not their apology.

Final Charge:

Quitting looks like strength.
Quarreling feels like power.
Quiet resentment seems like control.

But all three are prisons.

Stop letting unforgiveness stunt your life. Stop running. Stop fighting. Stop faking. Lay it down and *get your freedom back*.

Reflect, Release & Realign

What did this chapter reveal about your own heart?

Have you experienced this behavior or emotion in your own life? How has it affected you or others?

Who or what do you need to forgive—past or present—to break free from this?

What truth from God's Word stood out most in this chapter? How can you apply it?

What steps can you take this week to walk in forgiveness and healing?

R – Regret, Revenge, Rejection & Rehearsal of Pain: The Four Echoes of Unforgiveness

Scripture to Reflect On: 2 Corinthians 7:10, Romans 12:17, Isaiah 53:3

Unforgiveness has a ripple effect—it doesn't just stay in the moment of offense. It echoes through our lives in subtle, painful ways: through the regrets we carry, the revenge we crave, the healing we reject, and the pain we keep rehearsing. These four patterns rob us of peace and stunt our growth. They keep the wound open long after the offense has ended.

1. Unforgiveness doesn't whisper—it **echoes.**

> *"Godly sorrow brings repentance that leads to salvation and leaves no regret..."* — 2 Corinthians 7:10
> *"Do not repay anyone evil for evil..."* — Romans 12:17
> *"He was despised and rejected by men, a man of sorrows and acquainted with grief..."* — Isaiah 53:3

Some of y'all think the offense is over. But your *behavior* proves it isn't. Because now, your whole life is an echo chamber of the hurt you refused to heal. And that echo—regret, revenge, rejection, and rehearsal—is robbing you blind.

Unforgiveness is a ripple—it doesn't stay where it started. It spills over, staining your joy, your relationships, and even your faith.

2. The Four Echoes That Keep You Bound

Regret: What Was Lost Because You Wouldn't Let Go

Regret is the heavy sigh of *"I could've handled that better."*
It's the empty space where a relationship, an opportunity, or a season used to be—before your pride pushed it away.

Signs of Regret:

- "If only..." is your daily soundtrack
- You grieve relationships you ended out of anger
- Pride costs you time you can't get back
- You spend more time looking back than moving forward

Regret is the interest you pay on the debt of unforgiveness. Every year you don't forgive, the cost compounds.

Revenge: The Fire That Burns Both Ways

Revenge always promises satisfaction but delivers **bondage**.
Whether it's silent sabotage, gossip, or outright attack—you're drinking poison expecting them to die.

Signs of Revenge:

- Secretly celebrating their setbacks
- Retelling the story to destroy their reputation
- Withholding forgiveness to feel "powerful"
- Believing payback will fix your heart

Revenge doesn't give you justice—it gives you *joint*

pain with the devil. Because now, you're doing his work for him.

Rejection: Turning Away From Healing

Unforgiveness not only pushes people away—it pushes **healing** away.
You start rejecting God's attempts to restore you, and you call it "protection" when it's really *self-sabotage.*

Signs of Rejection:

- Avoiding honest conversations
- Distrusting people who actually care
- Feeling unworthy of love or restoration
- Ignoring God's invitation to peace

Some of you are rejecting the very answer to your prayer because it doesn't look like revenge.

Rehearsal of Pain: Playing the Tape That Keeps You Bound

You've become the star of your own trauma drama.
You can quote the offense word-for-word.
You tell the story like a testimony—but it's still a *tragedy.*

Signs of Rehearsal:

- Talking about it to anyone who will listen
- Reliving the pain in your head like it happened yesterday
- Using the hurt as your excuse for staying stuck
- Letting pain define your personality

As long as you keep rehearsing, God can't start

rewriting. Stop quoting the devil's script and start living God's story.

Choosing Redemption Over Repetition

1. **Acknowledge what you've lost** – Grieve it honestly. Your loss becomes wisdom when you let God touch it.

2. **Cancel the debt** – Not for them. For *you*. Forgiveness breaks the echo.

3. **Say yes to healing** – Stop rejecting the lifelines God is throwing you.

4. **Stop rehearsing. Start rewriting.** – Your pain is part of the story, but it's not the whole book. Start living in the next chapter.

Final Charge:

Regret will keep you in the past.
Revenge will chain you to pain.
Rejection will close the door on healing.
Rehearsal will make sure you *never move on.*

Unforgiveness is a broken record—and every time it spins, it scratches your soul. But grace has its own echo too. Forgive. Release. Heal. And let heaven's song be louder than hell's replay.

Reflect, Release & Realign

What did this chapter reveal about your own heart?

Have you experienced this behavior or emotion in your own life? How has it affected you or others?

Who or what do you need to forgive—past or present—to break free from this?

What truth from God's Word stood out most in this chapter? How can you apply it?

What steps can you take this week to walk in forgiveness and healing?

S – Sickness, Shame & Stagnation: The Cost of Carrying Pain Too Long

Scripture to Reflect On: James 5:16, Isaiah 61:7, Jeremiah 17:7–8

Unforgiveness doesn't just reside in the heart, but if not checked at the front door, it will spread. It seeps into the body, darkens the soul, and halts your progress in life. Left untreated, it can result in physical illness, internal shame, and the spiritual and emotional paralysis of stagnation. These three effects may not scream like anger or bitterness, but they quietly erode your health, identity, and destiny.

1. Unforgiveness doesn't just sit in your heart—it spreads like a virus.

> *"Confess your faults to one another and pray for one another, that you may be healed."* — James 5:16
> *"Instead of shame, you will receive a double portion..."* — Isaiah 61:7
> *"Blessed is the one who trusts in the Lord... they will be like a tree that does not wither."* — Jeremiah 17:7–8

You think you're just hurt. But your *body knows*. Your *spirit knows*. Your *future knows*. Pain that isn't released eventually finds another room to live in—your health, your identity, or your progress.

2. Sickness: When the Body Carries the Burden

Your heart can only hide pain for so long before your **body testifies against you**.

- Headaches that show up with memories
- Chest tightness when that name gets mentioned
- Fatigue that no nap can fix
- Insomnia when you're tired but not *at peace*

Some of y'all are praying for healing at the altar while holding the very weight that's making you sick. You don't need another pill—you need a *release*.

3. Shame: The Lie That You're Not Worth Healing

Unforgiveness eventually whispers:

- "You deserved this."
- "You're too broken to fix."
- "You'll never recover."

Shame doesn't just say *they hurt me*—it says *I must be the problem.*
It's the silent voice that keeps you hiding, self-sabotaging, and rejecting the very grace God is trying to pour out.

Signs of Shame:

- Negative self-talk
- Feeling unworthy of love or success
- Avoiding deep connection
- Struggling to accept blessings or compliments

The devil is a liar! You are not what they did. You are not what you lost. And you are not beyond redemption. The blood of Jesus doesn't just cover sin—it *cancels shame.*

4. Stagnation: When You're Alive But Not Advancing

Stagnation is the **quiet death of your destiny**. Unforgiveness freezes your forward motion:

- Dreams collect dust
- Faith feels mechanical
- Relationships plateau
- Life becomes survival instead of overflow

You're busy—but you're not *beating*. Your spirit has stopped moving because you're anchored to the moment they hurt you.

The Way Out

1. Care for your soul and body

Healing is holistic. Rest, hydrate, move, breathe. Your body deserves freedom as much as your heart does.

2. Renounce shame and embrace your worth

Speak life over yourself daily:

> "I am not what happened. I am loved. I am seen. I am chosen."

Shame dies the moment you expose it to **grace**.

3. Move—spiritually and practically

Even if it's small: pray again, laugh again, apply again, worship again.
Motion breaks the grip of stagnation.

4. Invite God into the hidden places

The sickness, the shame, the stuck places—those are the rooms He's been knocking on. Let Him in.

Final Charge:

Sickness will drain your health.
Shame will drain your identity.
Stagnation will drain your destiny.

And all three are symptoms of **pain that overstayed its welcome**.

You can't afford to keep carrying this.
Unforgiveness is charging you interest in your body, your soul, and your future. But the moment you release it; God will breathe life into places that have been silent for years. Forgive—so you can *finally live*.

Reflect, Release & Realign

What did this chapter reveal about your own heart?

Have you experienced this behavior or emotion in your own life? How has it affected you or others?

Who or what do you need to forgive—past or present—to break free from this?

What truth from God's Word stood out most in this chapter? How can you apply it?

What steps can you take this week to walk in forgiveness and healing?

T – Trapped in the Past, Turmoil, Torment & Trust Issues: When Yesterday Holds Today Hostage

Scripture to Reflect On: Philippians 3:13–14, Isaiah 26:3, Proverbs 3:5–6

Unforgiveness has a way of chaining us to moments we can't change. What was done may be over, but the impact lingers a little while, often times holding us hostage to the past, stirring up daily turmoil, tormenting us in silence, and making it nearly impossible to trust again. These are not just emotional wounds—they are life-altering strongholds.

1. Unforgiveness is the warden of your yesterday.

> *"Forgetting what is behind and straining toward what is ahead, I press on..."* — Philippians 3:13–14
> *"You will keep in perfect peace those whose minds are steadfast..."* — Isaiah 26:3
> *"Trust in the Lord with all your heart and lean not on your own understanding."* — Proverbs 3:5–6

Some of y'all aren't living—you're *looping*. The clock is moving, but your life is frozen in the moment they hurt you. Yesterday has a chokehold on your today, and you're calling it 'just how life is.' No, that's not life. That's **captivity**.

Unforgiveness is a **time machine** that only travels backwards.

2. Trapped in the Past: Living in the Loop of What Was

Unforgiveness keeps your mind hitting **replay**:

- You rehearse the scene
- You relive the words
- You re-feel the pain

Every time you think you've moved on, the enemy presses "Play" again.

Signs You're Trapped in the Past:

- Conversations always drift back to "what happened"
- New relationships suffer for old mistakes
- Life feels like it's moving, but *you're not*
- You hold people to the penalty of someone else's failure

You can't build your future while renting space to your past. You're still giving yesterday *free rent* in your spirit.

3. Turmoil: The Inner Storm That Never Settles

You can laugh, post selfies, and even shout in church— but your soul sounds like a thunderstorm.

Signs of Inner Turmoil:

- Mental overdrive and emotional fatigue
- Difficulty focusing, resting, or hearing from God
- Feeling "charged" with stress 24/7
- Sleep doesn't refresh because the storm didn't stop

You've learned to fake calm in public while drowning in private. But peace doesn't come from pretending—it comes from **forgiving.**

4. Torment: When Pain Haunts You

Torment is turmoil on steroids. It's pain that's been fed, nurtured, and *made a pet.*
It manifests as:

- Nightmares or flashbacks

- Mental harassment that won't let up

- Spiritual heaviness or oppression

- Feeling like God is distant, even when He's near

Torment is the rent you pay for squatting in unforgiveness. The devil doesn't need permission to whisper in your ear when you've already handed him the key.

5. Trust Issues: When Hurt Becomes Your Lens

After betrayal, your heart builds **walls instead of doors**.
And here's the trap: those walls don't just keep pain out—they keep love out too.

Signs of Trust Issues:

- Expecting betrayal before it happens

- Misreading kindness as manipulation

- Withholding your real self out of fear

- Sabotaging healthy relationships because of past hurt

You're punishing new people for old crimes.
You've locked the world out and called it 'wisdom,'

but it's really *woundedness* with a security system.

The Path to Release

1. Acknowledge where you're stuck

You can't get free from what you won't face. Name the wound. Name the person. Name the moment.

2. Confront the lies

Pain says, *"You'll never trust again. You'll never be safe. You'll never move forward."*
Forgiveness says, *"I may have been broken, but I am being rebuilt."*

3. Break the legal ground of torment

Pray. Forgive. Renounce the offense. Take back the territory the enemy squatted on.

When you release them, you evict the devil from your mind.

4. Relearn how to trust

Start small. Trust God first. Then let Him lead you to people who are safe.
Healing happens **one step, one yes, one open door at a time.**

Final Charge:

Trapped in the past.
Turmoil on the inside.
Torment in the night.
Trust issues in the day.

This is not the life God called you to live.

You can't drive forward staring in the rearview

mirror. Forgiveness doesn't change what they did—but it **changes what it can do to you.** Release the chains. Evict yesterday. And walk into the freedom your future is begging for.

Reflect, Release & Realign

What did this chapter reveal about your own heart?

Have you experienced this behavior or emotion in your own life? How has it affected you or others?

Who or what do you need to forgive—past or present—to break free from this?

What truth from God's Word stood out most in this chapter? How can you apply it?

What steps can you take this week to walk in forgiveness and healing?

U – Unhappiness, Unrest & Unworthiness: When Peace, Joy, and Identity Slip Away

Scripture to Reflect On: Isaiah 26:3, Romans 8:1, John 15:11, Psalm 139:14

Unforgiveness isn't just an emotional reaction—it's a joy thief, a peace disruptor, and an identity distorter. The longer it stays in your heart, the more quietly it rewrites how you live, what you believe about yourself, and how you experience the world around you. Through the dark lens of pain, happiness feels fake, rest feels unreachable, and worth feels unattainable.

1. Unforgiveness doesn't just hurt you—it rewrites you.

> *"You will keep in perfect peace those whose minds are steadfast, because they trust in you."* — Isaiah 26:3
> *"There is now no condemnation for those who are in Christ Jesus."* — Romans 8:1
> *"I have told you this so that my joy may be in you and that your joy may be complete."* — John 15:11
> *"I am fearfully and wonderfully made..."* — Psalm 139:14

You didn't notice it at first. But slowly, unforgiveness started siphoning your joy, disturbing your peace, and corroding your sense of worth. Now, happiness feels fake, rest feels impossible, and love feels undeserved. That's not your personality—that's a **soul under siege**.

2. Unhappiness: The Joy You Can't Touch

Unforgiveness is a joy thief. It doesn't just kill laughter—it puts joy on **mute**.

Signs You're Living in Unhappiness from Unforgiveness:

- Struggling to feel present in good moments
- Feeling guilty for smiling while still angry
- Reacting with irritation even during peaceful times
- Carrying a low-grade dissatisfaction everywhere you go

You can be in a room full of celebration and still feel empty. Why? Because joy can't breathe in a soul that's suffocating on yesterday.

3. Unrest: The Soul That Can't Settle

Unforgiveness is noisy. It plays **static** in your spirit 24/7:

- Racing thoughts that won't stop
- Restlessness even while you're resting
- Worship that feels blocked
- Prayers that feel distracted

You can't have the peace of God while you're still protecting the pain you refuse to give Him.

4. Unworthiness: The Lie That You're Not Enough

This is when the offense stops being something that *happened to you* and becomes something you believe *defines you*.

Signs of Unworthiness:

- Rejecting love because you feel undeserving
- Believing your purpose has expired because of what happened
- Thinking forgiveness must be earned
- Avoiding intimacy with God out of shame

That's the enemy's masterpiece—getting you to agree with your wound. But I came to remind you: **your worth is not on trial.** It was settled at the cross.

Returning to Wholeness

1. Reconnect with gratitude

Gratitude opens the window for joy to walk back in. Start small—thank Him for today, not yesterday's pain.

2. Create quiet space

You can't hear God over constant noise. Make room for stillness. Write. Worship. Walk. Breathe.

3. Speak truth over lies

Say it until your spirit believes it:

> "I am not what happened. I am loved. I am forgiven. I am chosen."

4. Let God restore your worth

You can't earn healing—you receive it. Sit in His presence until the shame loses its grip.

Final Charge:

Unhappiness will drain your smile.

Unrest will drain your sleep.
Unworthiness will drain your soul.

Unforgiveness is not just keeping you from others—it's keeping you from *you*. Forgive, not so they can be free, but so you can **remember who you are**.

Reflect, Release & Realign

What did this chapter reveal about your own heart?

Have you experienced this behavior or emotion in your own life? How has it affected you or others?

Who or what do you need to forgive—past or present—to break free from this?

What truth from God's Word stood out most in this chapter? How can you apply it?

What steps can you take this week to walk in forgiveness and healing?

V – Victim Mentality, Vengeance & Violence: The Triple Trap of Powerless Pain

Scripture to Reflect On: Romans 8:37, Proverbs 20:22, Ephesians 4:29

Unforgiveness doesn't just hurt you—it traps you. It tricks you into living as if you're still in the moment of offense. Over time, this creates a dangerous trio: the victim mentality that robs you of agency, the thirst for vengeance that keeps you angry, and the violence—emotional or verbal—that spills out onto others. These aren't just responses to hurt; they are ways pain tries to take control.

1. Unforgiveness doesn't just hurt you—it *hijacks you*.

> *"In all these things we are more than conquerors through Him who loved us."* — Romans 8:37
> *"Do not say, 'I will repay evil;' wait for the Lord, and He will deliver you."* — Proverbs 20:22
> *"Do not let any unwholesome talk come out of your mouths…"* — Ephesians 4:29

Pain has two goals: to make you powerless or to make you poisonous. Victim mentality keeps you weak. Vengeance keeps you angry. Violence spreads the infection to everybody else. That's the devil's three-step plan to destroy your destiny.

2. Victim Mentality: When Pain Becomes Your Identity

Being hurt is part of life. **Staying hurt is a choice.** A victim mentality tells you:

- "I can't move forward."
- "Nobody understands me."
- "I am what they did to me."

Signs of Victim Mentality:

- Rehearsing the wrongs daily
- Avoiding responsibility for your own healing
- Making decisions through the lens of past hurt
- Believing life is happening *to* you, not *through* you

You're not weak because you were wounded—
you're weak because you *keep wearing the wound
like it's your name tag*. God didn't call you
victim—He called you *more than a conqueror*.

3. Vengeance: The Desire to Wound Back

Revenge **feels righteous** in the moment, but it's just
recycled pain.
You want them to feel it.
You want them to see you rise.
You want the scales to balance.

Every time you plot payback, you're still playing
on the enemy's team. You can't heal holding the
sword of vengeance. The hand of vengeance and
the hand of victory are not the same hand.

Signs Vengeance Is Driving You:

- Fantasizing about their failure or humiliation
- Withholding love or kindness to "teach them"
- Needing to "win" at the cost of peace

- Refusing to release blame

4. Violence: When Pain Turns Outward

What you don't release will eventually **leak**—and often, it spills onto people who didn't even hurt you.

Forms of Unforgiveness-Fueled Violence:

- Sarcasm that cuts like knives

- Passive-aggressive jabs meant to punish

- Emotional manipulation, stonewalling, or coldness

- Explosive anger over minor triggers

Your pain is not just punishing you—it's *punching the people who love you most*. You can't weaponize your wound and still expect to walk in worship.

Pathway to Power and Peace

1. Reject the victim script

You didn't choose the pain, but you *can* choose the healing.

> "Stop letting someone else's actions narrate your life. Pick up the pen.

2. Release the right to get even

Forgiveness isn't about excusing them—it's about **evicting bitterness**.

God can settle the score better than you ever could.

3. Redirect your pain

Pour your pain into **purpose**. Mentor someone. Build something.
Turn your wound into **wisdom** and your hurt into **help** for others.

4. Speak life instead of death

Your tongue can either be a weapon or a well.
Choose words that heal, not harm. Declare restoration until your soul believes it.

Final Charge:

Victim mentality will leave you stuck.
Vengeance will leave you bitter.
Violence will leave you alone.

You are not a victim. You are not a vigilante. And you were never built for venom. You are a vessel of grace, healing, and authority. Forgiveness doesn't make you weak—it makes you *untouchable*. It takes your life out of the enemy's hands and puts it back in God's.

Reflect, Release & Realign

What did this chapter reveal about your own heart?

Have you experienced this behavior or emotion in your own life? How has it affected you or others?

Who or what do you need to forgive—past or present—to break free from this?

What truth from God's Word stood out most in this chapter? How can you apply it?

What steps can you take this week to walk in forgiveness and healing?

W – Wasted Time, Withholding Love & War Within: The Slow Erosion of a Life Unhealed

Scripture to Reflect On: Joel 2:25, 1 John 3:18, Romans 7:23–25

Unforgiveness is a thief that doesn't steal loudly—it drains quietly. It wastes your time, blocks the flow of love, and stirs up an inner war that never rests. You think you're protecting yourself from future pain, but in reality, you're forfeiting present peace. These three forces—wasted time, withheld love, and the war within—will leave you emotionally bankrupt if left unchecked.

1. Unforgiveness is the most expensive rent you'll ever pay—because it charges you in time, love, and peace.

> *"I will restore to you the years that the locust has eaten..."* — Joel 2:25
> *"Let us not love with words or speech but with actions and in truth."* — 1 John 3:18
> *"I see another law at work in me, waging war..."* — Romans 7:23

You think unforgiveness is just an emotion, but it's an embezzler. It's been stealing your hours, your relationships, and your sanity—and the worst part is, you *let it* because you thought you were in control.

2. Wasted Time: What You Lose While Holding On

Unforgiveness doesn't just keep you in pain—it **keeps you in place**.
The world moves forward, but you stay frozen in the

replay of the offense.

Signs of Wasted Time:

- Rehashing old arguments instead of planning your future

- Missing milestones because you were stuck in your head

- Promising yourself you'll "deal with it later" but never doing it

- Holding a grudge longer than the offense lasted

Some of y'all are still giving yesterday free rent while today's opportunities are passing you by. And here's the truth: you can't get those moments back. You can only **stop the bleeding now.**

3. Withholding Love: Guarding the Heart Too Tightly

The walls you build to keep pain out often **lock love out** too.
And here's the tragedy—you think you're protecting yourself, but you're really starving your own soul.

Signs You're Withholding Love:

- Keeping good people at a distance

- Avoiding emotional intimacy because "what if it happens again?"

- Making innocent people pay for someone else's mistake

- Feeling numb even in relationships you once cherished

You call it protection, but it's really punishment— both for them and for *you.* A heart that doesn't give love can't receive it either.

4. War Within: The Battle Between Healing and Holding On

This is the most **draining part**—the invisible fight nobody sees.
You want to heal.
You want to forgive.
But some part of you is still gripping the pain like it's power.

Signs of the Internal War:

- Feeling spiritually and emotionally exhausted

- Wanting to forgive but stuck in the cycle of anger

- Feeling guilty when you try to release it

- Living with a constant inner conflict that disturbs your peace

You are fighting a war that can only be won through surrender. The day you lay it down is the day you *win*.

The Way Forward

1. Redeem your time

Don't give pain another minute. Make a memory today. Take the trip. Call the person. Live forward.

2. Let love back in

Forgiveness reopens the heart. Start small. Let someone safe into the space pain has been renting.

3. Surrender the battle

Stop shadowboxing your own history. Lay it down. Let God fight the war you can't win alone.

4. Live forward, not backward

Stop counting what was lost and start multiplying what can be restored. Your future is still in front of you.

Final Charge:

Wasted time.
Withheld love.
War within.

Unforgiveness will drain all three until there's nothing left but **a life half-lived**.

The enemy doesn't need to destroy you loudly—he just needs you to *stay stuck quietly*. But today, you get to declare: **No more.** No more stolen days. No more locked-up love. No more inner war. I choose to forgive, and I choose to live.

Reflect, Release & Realign

What did this chapter reveal about your own heart?

Have you experienced this behavior or emotion in your own life? How has it affected you or others?

Who or what do you need to forgive—past or present—to break free from this?

What truth from God's Word stood out most in this chapter? How can you apply it?

What steps can you take this week to walk in forgiveness and healing?

X – X-Factor: The Invisible Costs of Unforgiveness

Scripture to Reflect On: Isaiah 43:19, Joshua 24:15, Hebrews 4:12 (Includes: eXit Wounds, Cross(X)-Roads, X-Ray Faith)

Not everything unforgiveness does is obvious. Some of its most destructive effects are hidden—beneath the surface, beneath your smile, beneath your faith walk. These are the X-factors: the hidden variables that quietly influence your health, relationships, spiritual life, and future. They manifest through unhealed eXit wounds, emotional Cross(X)-roads, and an internal need for X-Ray Faith to see what's truly going on inside.

1. Some of the deadliest effects of unforgiveness are the ones nobody sees.

> *"See, I am doing a new thing! Now it springs up; do you not perceive it?"* — Isaiah 43:19
> *"Choose this day whom you will serve..."* — Joshua 24:15
> *"The Word of God... judges the thoughts and attitudes of the heart."* — Hebrews 4:12

Not all pain screams. Some of it whispers. Some of it smiles on Sunday and bleeds on Monday. The most dangerous thing about unforgiveness isn't what you see—it's what's quietly **rewriting your life behind the scenes**.

He'd call these the **X-Factors**—the hidden variables shaping your joy, relationships, and destiny.

2. eXit Wounds: The People Who Left and the Pain That Stayed

Some of your deepest scars didn't come from the blow—they came from the **absence**.

- The one who walked away
- The friend who ghosted
- The family member who abandoned you without explanation

Unforgiveness keeps these wounds **fresh**, even years later.

Signs of Unhealed eXit Wounds:

- Lingering sadness over those who left without closure
- Fear of abandonment in new relationships
- Holding good people at arm's length to "play it safe"
- Anger or resentment toward people who never looked back

  You may not have bled on the outside, but your heart has been hemorrhaging ever since they left. Forgiveness isn't for them—it's so you stop dying in slow motion.

3. Cross(X)-Roads: The Choice Between Healing and Hurt

Every offense is a **crossroad moment**:
Do I release or replay?
Do I trust God or stay trapped?
Do I walk into my future or worship my pain?

Signs You're Stuck at the Cross(X)-Road:

- Repeating the same cycles in relationships
- Avoiding the hard but healing conversations
- Feeling torn between faith and fear
- Knowing what God is asking, but stalling anyway

Every day you delay forgiveness; you're making a choice—just not the one that leads to freedom. Your indecision is your decision.

4. X-Ray Faith: Seeing What's Really Broken

X-rays show **what the naked eye can't**.
X-Ray Faith says, *"God, show me the wounds I've buried so deep I can't even feel them anymore."*

Signs You Need X-Ray Faith:

- Functioning on the outside but fractured inside
- Numbness that can't be explained
- A buried story you can't seem to speak
- Fear of what healing might require, yet longing for peace

God doesn't scan your heart to shame you—He scans to **save you**. If you'll let Him expose it, He'll heal it.

The Way Through the Unknown

1. Name what's hidden

Call out the exits. Call out the pain. Call out the choice you've been avoiding.

Hell can't heal what you keep hiding. Drag it into the light.

2. Make the choice at the crossroads

Don't keep circling. Forgive. Release. Move forward.

Every time you forgive, you reroute your life
toward freedom.

3. Let God scan your heart

Invite Him to reveal what's broken and what's blocking
your peace.

God's X-ray is not exposure for punishment—it's
exposure for **deliverance**.

4. Turn your X-Factor into your testimony

What the enemy tried to bury will become the story
that frees someone else.
Your silent wound becomes a **spoken victory**.

Final Charge:

eXit wounds will bleed you dry.
Cross(X)-roads will paralyze your progress.
X-Ray Faith is your only way forward.

You can't heal what you won't face, and you can't
walk into new life carrying old death. Let God scan
it, fix it, and rewrite it. Forgive—and watch Him
turn your X-factor into your exodus.

Reflect, Release & Realign

What did this chapter reveal about your own heart?

Have you experienced this behavior or emotion in your own life? How has it affected you or others?

Who or what do you need to forgive—past or present—to break free from this?

What truth from God's Word stood out most in this chapter? How can you apply it?

What steps can you take this week to walk in forgiveness and healing?

Y – Yesterday's Yoke, Yearning for Closure & You vs. You: The Silent Struggle Within

Scripture to Reflect On: Galatians 5:1, Ecclesiastes 3:1, Romans 7:19–25

Unforgiveness doesn't just damage relationships—it damages *you*. It places a yoke on your shoulders that wasn't meant to be carried, fills your heart with unmet expectations, and turns your mind into a battlefield. These Y-factors—Yesterday's Yoke, Yearning for Closure, and the war of You vs. You—hold many people hostage long after the offense is over.

1. Some of y'all are free on paper—but in prison in your soul.

> *"It is for freedom that Christ has set us free. Stand firm, then, and do not let yourselves be burdened again by a yoke of slavery."* — Galatians 5:1
>
> *"There is a time for everything, and a season for every activity under the heavens."* — Ecclesiastes 3:1
>
> *"For I do not do the good I want to do... but it is sin living in me that does it."* — Romans 7:19

You can dress it up. You can shout over it. You can smile for the pictures. But unforgiveness has a **weight**—a yoke—that is bending your back and slowing your stride. And worse than the weight on your shoulders is the **war inside your spirit**.

2. Yesterday's Yoke: Carrying What You Were Meant to

Release

Unforgiveness **chains your today to your yesterday**. You're moving, but every step is heavy because you're dragging what you refuse to release.

Signs of Carrying Yesterday's Yoke:

- Emotional or spiritual heaviness without apparent reason

- Old pain dictating new decisions

- Inability to walk freely in joy, purpose, or calling

- Feeling exhausted even after rest

You're tired, not from what you're doing—but from what you're *dragging*. And as long as you carry what Christ already paid to remove, your spirit will stay out of breath.

3. Yearning for Closure: Waiting for What May Never Come

One of the greatest traps of unforgiveness is **delayed healing**—holding your freedom hostage until somebody else does what you think will fix you.

Signs You're Stuck Yearning for Closure:

- Rehearsing what you'd say if they came back

- Waiting on apologies or explanations that never come

- Feeling "unfinished" without their validation

- Believing you can't move on until they make it right

Closure is not a gift somebody gives you—it's a decision you give yourself. If you wait on them, you'll die waiting.

4. You vs. You: The Internal Tug-of-War

The most exhausting battle isn't with them—it's with **yourself**.
One version of you wants peace.
The other version clings to pain like it's protection.

Signs of the Inner War:

- Self-sabotage or cycles of guilt

- Emotional or spiritual conflict that never quiets

- Wanting freedom but avoiding the path to it

- Struggling to believe you even deserve healing

This is the hardest war to win—because you can't outrun yourself. You must confront the "*you*" that loves the pain as much as it hates it.

Breaking the Yoke and Winning the War

1. Lay Yesterday Down

Stop dragging what God has already delivered you from.

You can't run into your future carrying a casket from your past.

2. Create Your Own Closure

Write the letter you'll never send.
Pray the release.
Close the chapter—even if they never turn the page.

3. Silence the War Within

Speak life to yourself daily:

"I forgive. I release. I am free."
Freedom isn't a feeling first—it's a *decision*.

4. Yoke Yourself to Jesus

Trade your burden for His. He said His yoke is easy and His burden is light.

If you stay tied to the past, you'll stay tired in the present. Trade yokes.

Final Charge:

Yesterday's yoke will break your back.
Yearning for closure will break your hope.
You vs. You will break your peace.

Forgiveness is the only key that can unlock the cell you built for yourself. Stop waiting on them. Stop fighting you. Lay the weight down. Close the book. And walk out free.

Reflect, Release & Realign

What did this chapter reveal about your own heart?

Have you experienced this behavior or emotion in your own life? How has it affected you or others?

Who or what do you need to forgive—past or present—to break free from this?

What truth from God's Word stood out most in this chapter? How can you apply it?

What steps can you take this week to walk in forgiveness and healing?

Z – Zombie Living, Zero Peace, Zealous but Wounded & Zigzag Life: The Final Toll of Unforgiveness

Scripture to Reflect On: John 10:10, Isaiah 26:3, Romans 10:2–3, James 1:8

Unforgiveness is more than a feeling—it's a condition that affects how you live, how you love, and how you see yourself and God. If left unresolved, it pushes you into a state of spiritual paralysis and emotional chaos. This final chapter exposes four Z-factors that mark a soul imprisoned by pain: living like a Zombie, having Zero Peace, being Zealous but Wounded, and walking a Zigzag Life.

1. You made it to the end of the alphabet, but this is really the beginning of your freedom.

> *"The thief comes only to steal and kill and destroy; I have come that they may have life and have it more abundantly."* — John 10:10
> *"You will keep in perfect peace those whose minds are steadfast..."* — Isaiah 26:3
> *"They are zealous for God, but their zeal is not based on knowledge."* — Romans 10:2–3
> *"A double minded man is unstable in all his ways."* — James 1:8

If unforgiveness had its way, this is where it would leave you—breathing but not alive, moving but not progressing, talking about God while dying inside, and stumbling in circles. And if we're honest, some of y'all have been living in this Z-zone for years.

2. Zombie Living: Walking but Not Alive

Unforgiveness numbs you into *existence without life.*
You're clocking in, showing up, smiling when needed—
but your soul is on autopilot.

Signs You're Living Like a Zombie:

- Emotional detachment from moments that should matter

- Going through motions without passion

- Numb to worship, love, or laughter

- Unexplained exhaustion

You've got a pulse but no purpose. That's not life—
that's spiritual hospice. And Jesus didn't die for
you to walk around like a well-dressed corpse.

3. Zero Peace: The Complete Absence of Rest

You can't have peace where offense is king.
Restlessness becomes your normal. Silence becomes
uncomfortable. Even in stillness, your soul won't stop
buzzing.

Signs of Zero Peace:

- Irritability in calm moments

- Persistent anxiety or mental noise

- Feeling emotionally clenched all the time

- Inability to be still without agitation

The devil doesn't even have to attack—he just lets
you replay the offense until you've worn your own
peace out.

4. Zealous but Wounded: Passion Covered in Pain

You can be on fire *for* God and still be bleeding *inside*. You work hard, serve long, and preach loud—but your drive is part ministry, part coping mechanism.

Signs of Zealous but Wounded:

- Using service to distract from your own healing
- Overextending to prove your worth
- Burnout masked as "just being busy for the Lord"
- Struggling to receive love or rest

Your zeal is real, but it's contaminated. God doesn't just want what you can *do*—He wants you *whole*.

5. Zigzag Life: No Clear Path, Just Survival

When unforgiveness runs the show, your steps have no straight line.
One day you want freedom, the next you retreat into pain. You're always moving—but never arriving.

Signs of a Zigzag Life:

- Inconsistent spiritual discipline
- Constant course changes with no breakthrough
- Perpetual feelings of being stuck
- Living reactively instead of with God-given direction

That instability isn't because God isn't speaking—it's because you keep changing the channel between His voice and your offense.

From Z-Factor to Zero Chains

1. Choose life over survival

Stop settling for numb existence. Invite joy and hope back in—on purpose.

2. Pursue peace like a promise

Peace is not going to hunt you down. You go get it by releasing what's been stealing it.

3. Heal the zeal

Let your service flow from a healed place, not a hidden wound.

4. Walk straight, not scattered

Forgiveness stabilizes your steps. It clears the fog and gives you forward focus.

Final Charge:

Zombie Living will drain your life.
Zero Peace will drain your mind.
Zealous but Wounded will drain your ministry.
Zigzag Life will drain your destiny.

You've reached Z. This is the alphabet's end—but it's heaven's beginning for you. Forgiveness isn't just a command—it's a jailbreak. Lay it all down. Let God resurrect your joy, your peace, your purpose. From A to Z, let this be your testimony: **I am free, and I am fully alive.**

Reflect, Release & Realign

What did this chapter reveal about your own heart?

Have you experienced this behavior or emotion in your own life? How has it affected you or others?

Who or what do you need to forgive—past or present—to break free from this?

What truth from God's Word stood out most in this chapter? How can you apply it?

What steps can you take this week to walk in forgiveness and healing?

Conclusion: Where the Chains Break and the Soul Breathes Again

If you've made it to this point, then you've walked through the entire alphabet of what unforgiveness can do and it's not just theory. It's real. It's raw. And if you were honest with yourself while reading, then maybe you saw pieces of *you* in these pages.

Maybe you recognized your smile masking a Zombie life. Maybe you saw your bitterness disguised as boldness. Maybe your heart raced when you read about regret, rejection, or revenge—because deep down, that's been you. Maybe you realized how many years, how many relationships, how much joy you've forfeited by gripping tightly to pain.

Unforgiveness is not just a spiritual issue, it's a soul cancer. It eats away at your vision. It poisons your purpose. It depletes your energy and distorts your identity. It's not passive. It's aggressive. And if left unaddressed, it will kill everything beautiful inside of you. Slowly. Quietly. Completely.

But this isn't the end of your story.

This is your wake-up call.

You don't need another sermon, another quote, or another excuse. What you need is to decide. Right here. Right now. Decide that you are no longer going to live shackled by what someone did to you or what you did to someone else. Decide that you will no longer be a slave to the past, a prisoner of pain, or a worshipper in chains.

Forgiveness isn't forgetting. It isn't pretending. It's not a denial of justice; it's a surrender of control. It's trusting that God is better at healing and judging than you are at holding grudges. It's releasing the weight that was never yours to carry in the first place.

You cannot change the past, but you can absolutely change the grip it has on you.

So, here's the final question: Will you continue to drag around the corpse of what hurt you? Or will you finally bury it, rise up, and walk in the resurrection of your own healing?

Forgiveness is not for the weak—it's the weapon of the truly free. And freedom is not a fantasy—it's your inheritance.

Lay down your letter.
Break the chain.
Breathe again.

This is the end of the alphabet, but the beginning of your new life.

Reflection Questions for Your Healing Journey

1. Which "letter" of unforgiveness hit you the hardest? Why?

2. What have you been holding onto that God has been asking you to release?

3. Who do you need to forgive, not for their sake, but for your own freedom?

4. In what ways has unforgiveness shaped your identity, relationships, or decisions?

5. What does true peace look like for you and what's standing in the way?

6. Have you mistaken survival for healing? What would true healing look like?

7. Are you willing to trust God with your pain and your justice?

8. What steps can you take today to begin walking in forgiveness?

Prayer of Release and Restoration

Heavenly Father,

Today, I make a decision that I no longer want to carry what You've already given me permission to release. I bring You every wound, every offense, every betrayal, every memory that's kept me bound. I confess that unforgiveness has lived in my heart and it has poisoned my peace. But I declare now: no more.

I forgive. I release. I let go.

Not because they earned it. Not because it makes sense. But because You first forgave me. And because freedom is mine through Christ.

Heal me where I'm broken. Mend what's been torn. Renew what's been wasted. Restore what I thought was lost forever. I renounce bitterness, anger, shame, and every identity I've worn that wasn't born of Your love. From this moment forward, I am not a prisoner of pain. I am a vessel of purpose. In Jesus' name, I walk in forgiveness, freedom, and full healing. Amen.

Are you ready to heal from what they did and who you became because of it?

Then turn the page. Freedom has been waiting for you.

Declaration of Freedom

I am not my past.
I am not their offense.
I am not the lie that unforgiveness told me.

I am healed. I am whole. I am free.

Today, I choose peace.
Today, I choose healing.
Today, I choose forgiveness.

My soul breathes again. My spirit rises again.
And my life begins again...today!

Amen.